METAMORPHIC ROCKS

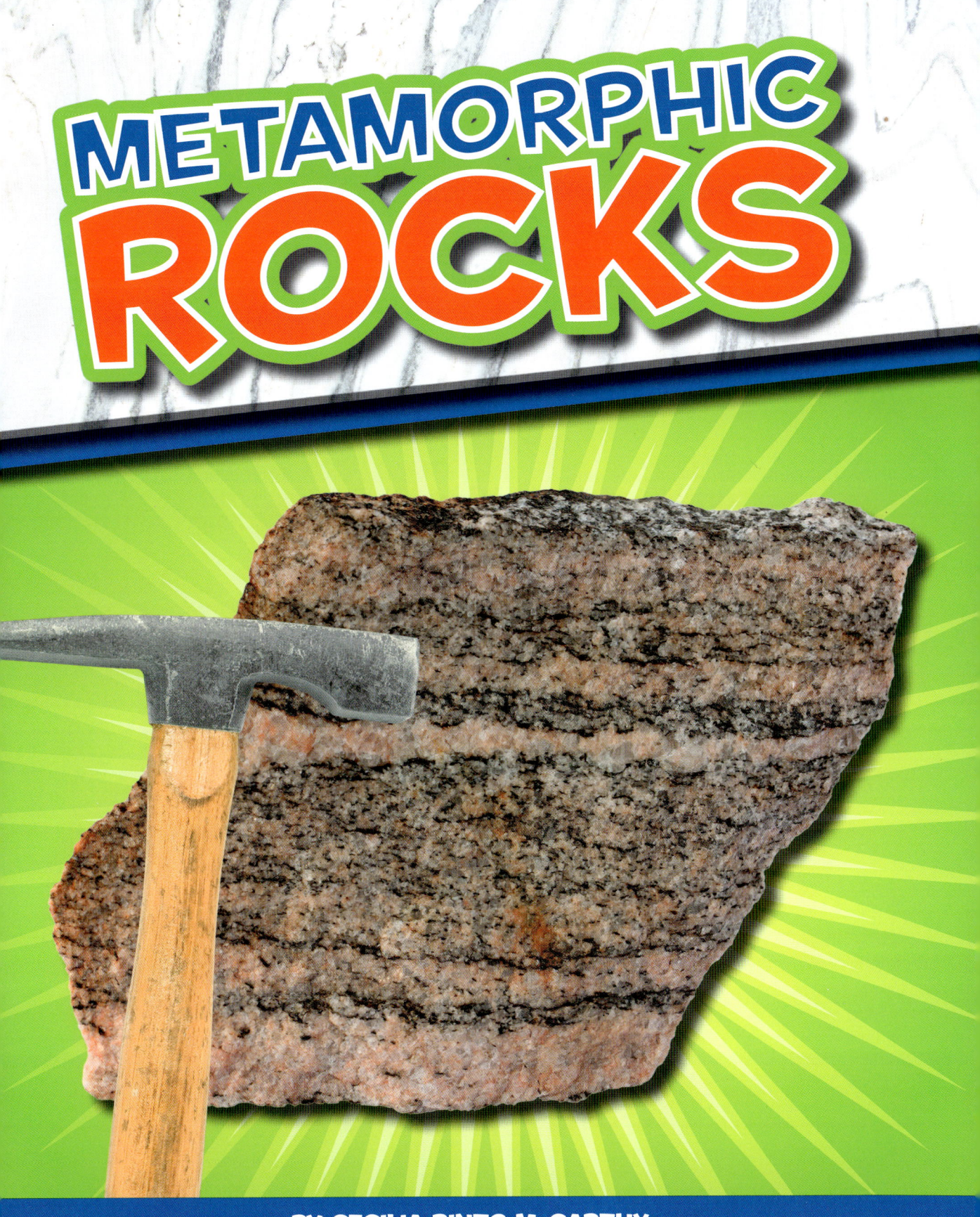

BY CECILIA PINTO McCARTHY

Published by The Child's World®
1980 Lookout Drive • Mankato, MN 56003-1705
800-599-READ • www.childsworld.com

Acknowledgments
The Child's World®: Mary Swensen, Publishing Director
Red Line Editorial: Editorial direction and production
The Design Lab: Design

Design Element: Shutterstock images
Photographs ©: Shutterstock Images, cover (top), cover (bottom right), 1 (top), 1 (bottom right), 14, 15, 19, 20, 23; iStockphoto, cover (bottom left), 1 (bottom left), 4, 9, 11; Aaron Rutten/Shutterstock Images, 6; Mihail Ulianikov/Shutterstock Images, 7; Tyler Boyes/Shutterstock Images, 8, 13; Noppadon Sangpeam/Shutterstock Images, 16; Kerstin Waurick/iStockphoto, 17

Copyright © 2017 by The Child's World®
All rights reserved. No part of this book may be reproduced or utilized in any form or by any means without written permission from the publisher.

ISBN 9781503808027
LCCN 2015958143

Printed in the United States of America
Mankato, MN
June, 2016
PA02305

ABOUT THE AUTHOR

Cecilia Pinto McCarthy has always been fascinated by the natural world. She writes about science and nature and teaches natural history classes at a nature sanctuary. McCarthy enjoys hiking, nature photography, and hunting for fossils. She lives north of Boston with her family.

CONTENTS

CHAPTER 1
What Are Metamorphic Rocks?...4

CHAPTER 2
Making Metamorphic Rocks...8

CHAPTER 3
Kinds of Metamorphic Rocks...12

CHAPTER 4
Uses for Metamorphic Rocks...17

GLOSSARY...22

TO LEARN MORE...23

INDEX...24

CHAPTER 1

What Are Metamorphic Rocks?

Our planet is made mostly of rock. Rocks cover Earth's surface. You can find them under the oceans and deep beneath the soil. Rocks are part of everyday life. Each day, people drink from glasses. They use toothpaste and write with pencils. All of these products are made from rocks.

Geologists study rocks. They sort rocks into groups based on how the rocks form. There are many

Quartzite is a metamorphic rock. It forms from the sedimentary rock sandstone.

different kinds of rocks. The three main groups are igneous, sedimentary, and metamorphic.

Metamorphic comes from a Greek word for "change." Metamorphic rocks are made from other rocks that have changed form. These **parent rocks** may be igneous or sedimentary rocks. They can even be other metamorphic rocks. Metamorphic rocks look different from their parent rocks. They can have different colors and textures. But they are made of the same **elements**.

Most metamorphic rocks form deep underground. Earth is made of different layers. The top layer is called the crust. Below the crust is a thicker layer called the mantle. **Magma** from the mantle rises toward the crust. As it rises, it heats up rocks. The heat affects **minerals** in rocks.

IGNEOUS AND SEDIMENTARY ROCKS

Igneous rocks form from magma. As magma cools, it hardens into rock. Igneous rock is often found near volcanoes. Sedimentary rocks are made from natural materials. They are created from layers of rock, mud, and plant material. The formation process is slow. It can take millions of years for rock to form.

LAYERS OF EARTH

Earth has four layers. The top layer is the crust. This layer ranges from 3 to 30 miles (8 to 48 km) thick. The mantle is thicker. It is made of hot rock. Earth's core is made of two elements, iron and nickel. In the outer core, these elements are in a liquid state. In the inner core, these elements are in a solid state.

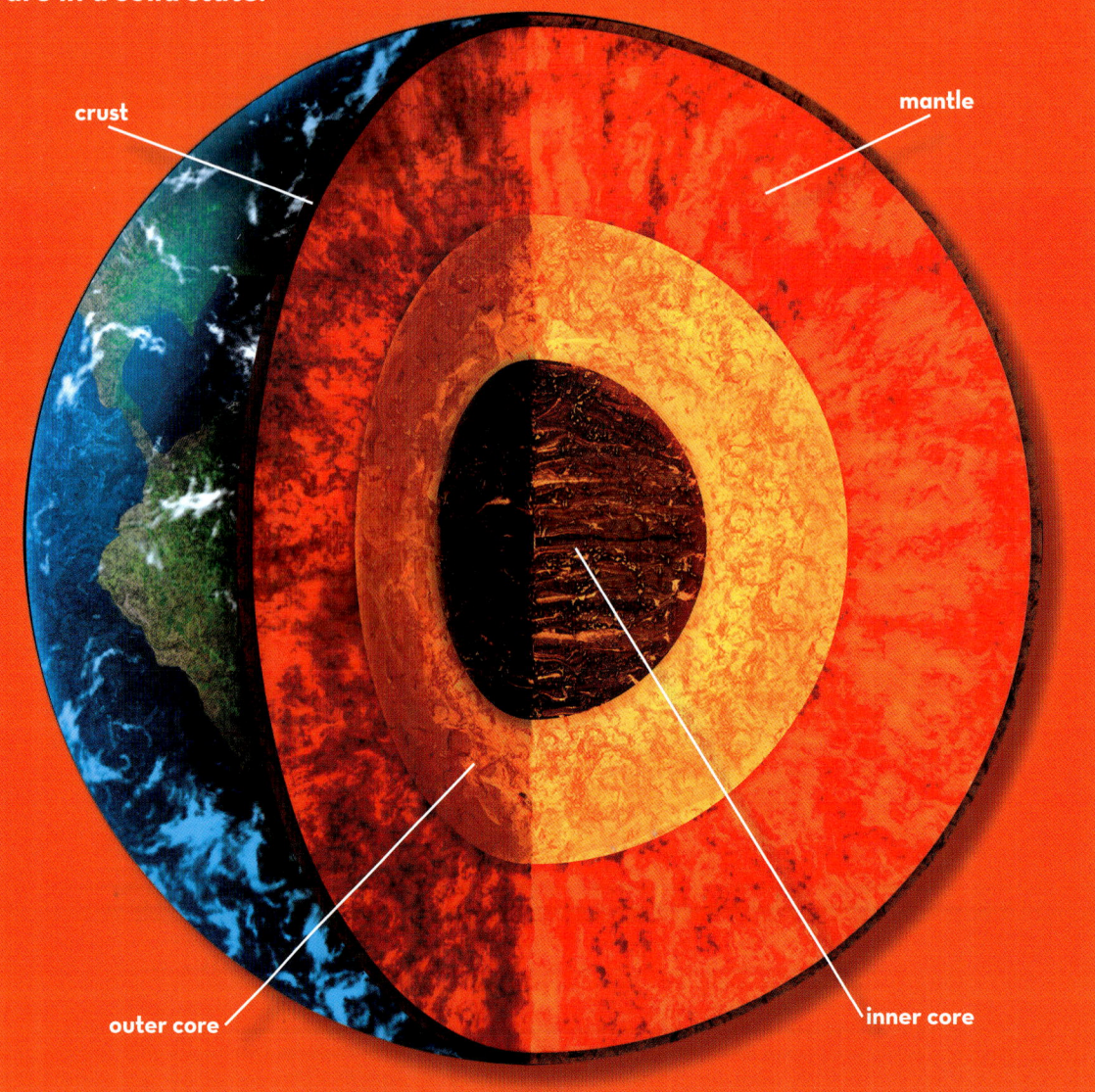

crust

mantle

outer core

inner core

All rocks are made of minerals. Some rocks contain only two minerals. Others contain many more. The minerals are made of elements. Under extreme heat and pressure, the minerals break down. The elements combine in different ways. They form new minerals. This process creates new rocks.

Heat and pressure form all metamorphic rocks. This process is called metamorphism. Different types of metamorphism form different types of rocks.

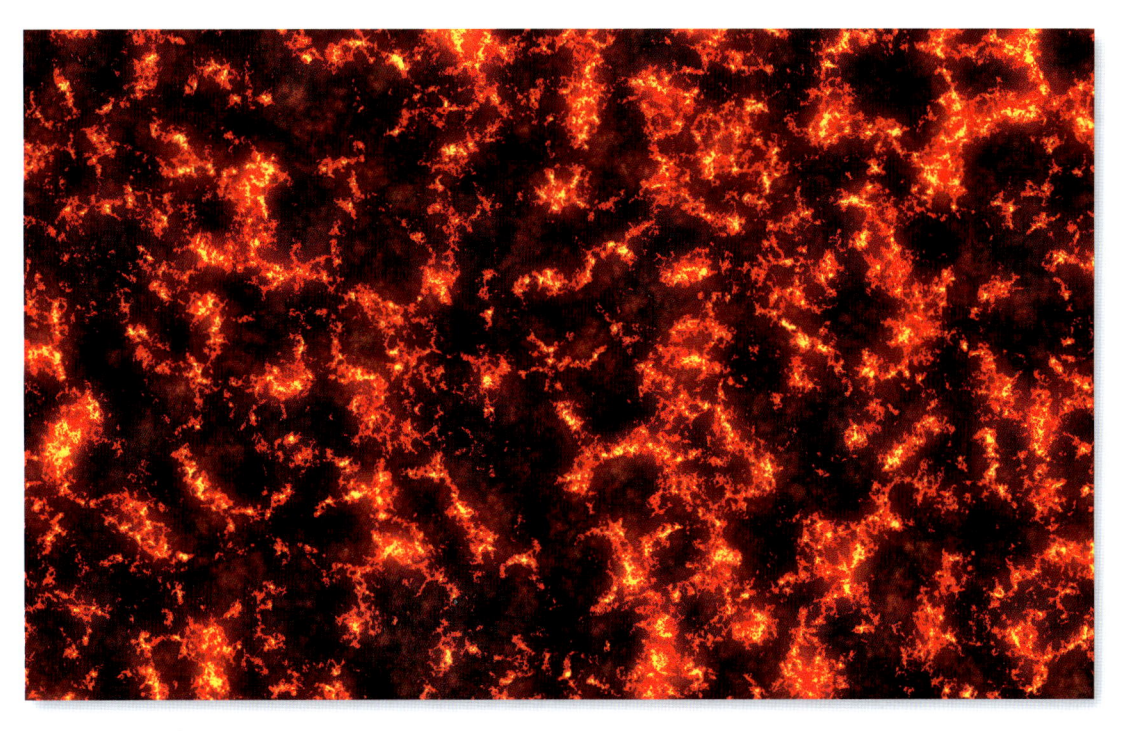

Magma under Earth's surface can heat up nearby rocks, forming metamorphic rock.

CHAPTER 2

Making Metamorphic Rocks

Beneath Earth's surface, heat and pressure put stress on rocks. Top layers of rock press down on the bottom layers. Hot magma flows upward. The heat and pressure change parent rocks into metamorphic rock. This change can happen in different ways.

One way is through contact metamorphism. During this process, magma enters areas called **intrusions**. Empty spaces in the intrusions fill with magma. The trapped magma heats up nearby rock. It causes a change in the minerals of the rock. Contact metamorphism affects only limited areas near the magma. These areas are up to 6 miles

Slate, a smooth gray or black rock, forms through contact metamorphism.

(10 km) wide. Marble and slate are both formed by contact metamorphism.

Another way is through regional metamorphism. During this process, extreme pressure and heat affect a large area of the crust. Often, the movement of Earth's tectonic plates causes regional metamorphism.

Tectonic plates are giant slabs of solid rock. These slabs make up Earth's crust. Regional metamorphism often occurs at a **subduction zone**. This is a place where plates meet. Sometimes, one plate slips under another. Extreme pressure occurs in this area. Rocks such as eclogite and blueschist form in subduction zones.

Eclogite is one rock that can form in subduction zones.

SHOCK METAMORPHISM

Not all metamorphic rocks take years to form. Sometimes a meteorite crashes to Earth. A meteorite is a rock from space. The impact makes a hole called a crater. The crash creates intense heat and force. It changes the nearby rocks. They quickly become metamorphic rock. This process is called shock metamorphism.

Tectonic plates can also **collide**. Crashing plates squeeze nearby rocks. The rocks deform and fold. As they press together, they form new rocks. The pressure can push rocks up to the surface. Over millions of years, the rising rocks become mountains. Mountain ranges often contain many metamorphic rocks.

A third process is known as dynamic metamorphism. During this process, tectonic plates slide over one another. They move in opposite directions. Large cracks called **faults** open in the crust. The temperature of the faults is often low. But there is enough pressure to make metamorphic rock. Rocks called mylonites form through dynamic metamorphism.

Metamorphic rocks usually form very slowly. The process often takes thousands of years. Many rocks take millions of years to form. People cannot see this process

Some faults are visible on Earth's surface. The pressure near the faults can form metamorphic rocks.

directly. But the rocks contain clues. These clues help scientists determine how each rock formed.

CHAPTER 3

Kinds of Metamorphic Rocks

Metamorphic rocks can form in different ways. Often, their traits show how the rocks formed. Scientists study different rock traits. These traits help them learn when a rock formed. Scientists can also determine the amounts of heat and pressure that the rock was under.

Geologists look for several qualities in rocks. One is the type of crystals. These crystals are grains of minerals in the rock. Crystals contain **atoms** of different elements in an organized structure. Metamorphic rocks can have large or small crystals. Sometimes, the temperature increases while a rock is forming. This increase often causes small crystals to form. If the temperature stays the same, larger crystals are more likely.

Metamorphic rocks also have a variety of textures. They can be fine, medium, or coarse. Rocks include grains or particles of different minerals. Scientists study the size of the grains. Rocks with a fine texture have small

Phyllite is one example of a foliated rock.

grains. Rocks with a coarse texture have large grains. The size and organization of the grains help show how a rock formed.

Foliated rocks have layers. Most foliated rocks are formed by heavy pressure. These rocks usually contain many minerals. The different minerals often look like stripes or lines. The lines of minerals make layers. Sometimes, the lines curve or bend. Some foliated rocks look folded. Slate, schist, and gneiss are all foliated rocks.

Temperatures affect a foliated rock's texture. The higher the temperature when the rock was formed, the higher the **grade** of a rock. Grades can be low, medium, or high. Low-grade rocks are formed at temperatures from 390 to 610 degrees Fahrenheit (200 to 320°C).

Gneiss, a high-grade rock, has large, coarse grains.

These rocks usually have fine grains. High-grade rocks form at higher temperatures. The highest-grade rocks can form at temperatures of 1290 degrees Fahrenheit (700°C). They have coarse grains.

Slate is a low-grade rock. It is made from the sedimentary rock shale. Slate has many layers. But its grains are very small. They are hard to see. Schist is a medium-grade rock. It is formed under higher temperature and pressure than slate. The grains in schist are sometimes difficult to see, too. They become visible under the light. Gneiss is a high-grade rock. It is formed under extreme heat and pressure. It has coarse grains that are easy to see.

Nonfoliated rocks do not have layers. The minerals in the rocks are not arranged in a regular pattern. These rocks usually form through contact metamorphism. High heat affects the parent rock, rearranging the minerals.

The heat also removes water from the parent rock. The result is a rock with tightly packed atoms. Nonfoliated rocks are some of the hardest rocks.

Nonfoliated rocks are made of just a few minerals. Hornfels is one example. It contains the minerals chlorite, biotite, and hornblende. Some early humans used this rock to make tools. Its hardness made it difficult to break. Hornfels is still found today in the southern United States.

SLATE FOSSILS

Fossils are not often found in metamorphic rock. They are usually crushed by the temperatures and pressures that form the rock. Some fossils are found in slate. Slate deposits are often found in Hunsrück, Germany. The Hunsrück slate contains hundreds of fossils. Some of these fossils are nearly 400 million years old.

Hornfels is a hard nonfoliated rock. This one contains brown spots from fossils of ammonites, a type of mollusk.

Marble is another nonfoliated rock. Most marble is made from a sedimentary rock called limestone. The main mineral in marble is calcite. Pure white marble contains only the mineral calcite. But marble usually contains other minerals, too. These other minerals add color to marble. Colored marble can be pink, green, or black.

Like hornfels, marble is a useful rock. It is sturdy enough for use in construction. Artists appreciate its colors and patterns. Metamorphic rocks have many uses in everyday life.

The patterns and smooth texture of marble make it a popular building material.

CHAPTER 4

Uses for Metamorphic Rocks

All rocks contain valuable information. Rocks help geologists learn about Earth's history. Metamorphic rocks tell scientists how tectonic plates move. They provide clues for how mountain ranges form. This information helps scientists understand the world. Based on Earth's past, they predict what could happen in the future. Rocks are an important natural resource.

Metamorphic rocks are useful in other ways, too. They are a source of gemstones and minerals. Garnets are one type of gemstone. They are mainly found in metamorphic rock. Some garnets are bright red. They are often used in jewelry.

Garnets, often found in metamorphic rock, are commonly used in jewelry.

SLATE IN SCHOOLS

During the 1800s, schools did not use paper. Instead, children wrote on flat pieces of slate. They used chalk to write. The slate was easy to wipe clean. People still say, "Start with a clean slate." This saying means to forget past mistakes and start again.

Metamorphic rocks are also used to construct buildings. Slate is mined around the world. Some is found in the United States. It also comes from Wales and Spain. Slate splits easily into flat sheets. It is hard and sturdy. Slate is a perfect material for patio tiles. Roof shingles are often made of slate. Slate roofing can last for more than 100 years.

Gneiss is another important building material. This rock crushes easily. Crushed gneiss is used to construct roads. Gneiss can also be cut into slabs. The slabs are used to make stairs and countertops. Minerals found in gneiss are also useful. Graphite is found in gneiss. This mineral is used in pencils. Gneiss is usually formed from granite, an igneous rock. It can also come from a metamorphic rock called schist. Schist is another useful rock. It is used to make floors.

Marble is prized for its hardness and beauty. White Carrara marble comes from the Apuan Alps in Italy.

The Lincoln Memorial contains several types of marble.

This marble is easy to cut and polish. It is often used for sculptures. Many artists have carved statues from Carrara marble.

Marble is also used in monuments. The Lincoln Memorial is located in Washington, DC. This monument is made from several different types of marble. The statue of Lincoln is made from white Georgia marble. The floor is pink marble from Tennessee. The stairs include marble blocks from Colorado.

The Taj Mahal in India was built with white marble.

People have used marble for many years. India's Taj Mahal was built in the 1600s. An emperor built the majestic building as a tomb. It is made of white marble. Each year, millions of people visit the Taj Mahal.

Marble has a wide range of uses. The mineral calcium carbonate is found in marble. It is used in paints and toothpaste. Ground marble is even used in cleaning supplies.

METAMORPHIC ROCKS AND THEIR PARENT ROCKS

Metamorphic Rock	Parent Rock(s)
slate	shale, mudstone, or siltstone
marble	limestone or dolostone
quartzite	quartz sandstone
gneiss	granite or schist
phyllite	slate
schist	phyllite
eclogite	shale

Most metamorphic rocks were formed long ago. They show what the Earth was like in the past. But they are still important today. People use metamorphic rocks to make buildings and roads. Artists use them to create statues and jewelry. Many materials from metamorphic rocks improve our lives. We use them every day.

GLOSSARY

atoms *(AT-uhmz)* Atoms are the smallest parts of an element that have all the properties of the element. Atoms of different elements combine to form crystals.

collide *(kuh-LIED)* To collide is to crash together with great force. Some metamorphic rocks form in places where tectonic plates collide.

elements *(EL-uh-muhnts)* Elements are substances that cannot be broken into a simpler substance. When metamorphic rocks form, they have the same elements as the original rocks.

faults *(FAWLTS)* Faults are places on Earth's surface where tectonic plates meet. Metamorphic rocks can form near faults.

foliated *(FOH-lee-ayt-ed)* When something is foliated, it has layers. Slate is a foliated rock that splits into many flat layers.

geologists *(jee-OL-uh-jists)* Geologists are scientists who study rocks. Geologists might analyze a metamorphic rock to learn how old it is.

grade *(GRAYD)* Grade is a measurement of the temperature and pressure that form a metamorphic rock. Rocks with a low grade are formed under low temperature and pressure.

intrusions *(in-TROO-zhuns)* Intrusions are large underground formations of igneous rocks. Heat from magma near intrusions can form metamorphic rock.

magma *(MAG-muh)* Magma is hot melted rock from inside Earth. When magma cools, it forms rock.

minerals *(MIN-ur-uhlz)* Minerals are substances found in nature that are not animals or plants. A rock may contain many minerals.

parent rocks *(PAIR-unt ROKS)* Metamorphic rocks form from parent rocks. The parent rocks may be igneous, sedimentary, or other metamorphic rocks.

subduction zone *(sub-DUK-shun ZOHN)* The subduction zone is the place where two tectonic plates crash or meet. The pressure and heat at a subduction zone can create metamorphic rocks.

TO LEARN MORE

IN THE LIBRARY

Allen, Nancy Kelly. *Slate and Other Metamorphic Rocks*. New York: PowerKids, 2009.

Aloian, Molly. *What Are Metamorphic Rocks?* New York: Crabtree, 2011.

Dee, Willa. *Unearthing Metamorphic Rocks*. New York: PowerKids, 2014.

Nelson, Maria. *Metamorphic Rocks*. New York: Gareth Stevens, 2014.

ON THE WEB

Visit our Web site for links about metamorphic rocks: **childsworld.com/links**

Note to Parents, Teachers, and Librarians: We routinely verify our Web links to make sure they are safe and active sites. So encourage your readers to check them out!

INDEX

atoms, 12, 15

calcite, 16
contact metamorphism, 8–9, 14

dynamic metamorphism, 10

eclogite, 9, 21
elements, 5, 6, 7, 12

foliated rocks, 13
fossils, 15

garnets, 17
geologists, 4, 12, 17
gneiss, 13, 14, 18, 21
graphite, 18

hornfels, 15, 16

igneous rocks, 5, 18
intrusions, 8

layers of Earth, 5, 6
Lincoln Memorial, 19

magma, 5, 8
marble, 9, 16, 18–20, 21

nonfoliated rocks, 14–16

parent rocks, 5, 8, 14, 15, 21
phyllite, 13, 21

regional metamorphism, 9

sandstone, 21
schist, 13, 14, 18, 21
sedimentary rocks, 5, 14, 16
shale, 14, 21
shock metamorphism, 10
slate, 9, 13, 14, 15, 18, 21
subduction zone, 9

Taj Mahal, 20
tectonic plates, 9, 10, 17